creative journey of bipolar disorder

roz long

Creative Journey of Bipolar Disorder

Copyright © 2012 by Roz Long

Cover artwork and design by Ashley Good.

ISBN-13: 978-1478340058
ISBN-10: 1478340053

To my children, Scottie and Ryan.
May there be understanding and hope for those in need.

god's mix

If I were a painter
I would paint a picture
This day into evening

Tall trees silhouette the sky
Beautiful colors that have no names
Colors I know I could not mix

Maybe they were mixed by God

Two little birds cross the sky
I envy their freedom
So simply they flutter and float

If I were a poet
I would find some succinct way
To suppose their mutual joy

The birds are probably just looking for some worms

I am not sure what I am doing

In God's Mix

— John Kastholm

author's note

Everyone knows someone who is bipolar: a friend, lover, husband, wife, brother, sister, father, mother, son, daughter, aunt, uncle, cousin, nephew, niece, teacher, actor, actress, playwright, poet, artist, dancer, musician, architect, boss, celebrity, etc. ...

But does everyone or anyone know what bipolar disorder is?

Does everyone or anyone know that there is a high correlation between creativity and bipolar disorder?

The National Institute of Mental Health has published a detailed booklet that describes bipolar symptoms, causes, and treatments with information on getting help and coping. "Bipolar disorder, also known as manic depressive illness, causes unusual shifts in mood, energy, activity levels, and the ability to carry out day-to-day tasks. Symptoms of bipolar disorder are severe. They are different from the normal ups and downs that everyone goes through from time to time. Bipolar disorder symptoms can result in damaged relationships, poor job or school performance, and even suicide. But bipolar disorder can be treated, and people with this illness can lead full and productive lives. Bipolar disorder often develops in a person's late teens or early adult years. At least half of all cases begin before age 25. Some people have their first symptoms during childhood, while others may develop symptoms late in life. Bipolar disorder is not easy to detect when it starts. The symptoms may seem like separate problems, not recognized as part of a larger problem. Some people suffer for years before they are properly diagnosed and treated. Like diabetes or heart disease, bipolar disorder is a long-term illness that must be carefully managed throughout a person's life."

I want to share this book with you so that you will begin to realize that having the disease bipolar disorder not only causes pain and challenges but also inspires creativity for a high percentage of this population. With patience, understanding, medical help, and therapy, people who live with bipolar disorder can lead a good life.

Some of my former students and dear friends live with this disease. They continue to inspire me with the artistic journey of my life. I thank them for that.

— Roz Long

table of contents

the last leaf

As I began to write in my journal, I noticed the last few leaves of the oak tree out front flying against my window. Fall would end soon. I felt so alone. My mind suddenly flooded with thoughts of Clint. I missed him.

Clint, a former student, lived in a world where he believed no one would understand his depressed state. He believed that the world would one day self-destruct. Society would destroy itself. No love of life, no dreams, no support, no family, no sounds of laughter. There was only noise. The noise of guns, of rivalry between family members, of conflict between citizens, and of international strife between nations. A lack of trust that weakened humanity's soul.

He was a tender young man who lived in the wrong decade. His soulful mind belonged in the sixties with The Doors, Grateful Dead, Hendrix, Joplin, and the Moody Blues. He was lost in a world of unfaithful people. He was a vision to behold, dressed in the attire of the 1960s movement with his bell-bottom blue jeans, sixties peace necklace, macramé bracelet, and shoulder-length hair.

I was privileged and honored to share some time with him. We shared a mystical part of each other. Our destiny was found within the joining of our souls. His was a youthful spirit that will remain alive throughout time. Time can be held for a moment, but the value of friendship will be held eternally. The fond memories of our communication will never die. Love will endure. Those recollections will survive the hands of time. Love will protect.

the wall

One eventful day in the fall, I met a student in prison who would change my life forever, a youthful spirit who disliked the world for aging him. A child who abandoned his family because they had abandoned him. A heart so full of warmth that the heat that exuded from his presence could set me on fire. A caring individual who would love like no one.

As I walked into one of the rooms where I would be tutoring him in English for the first time, I sensed his pain of loneliness. The surroundings were dark and full of despair. No windows to share the outside light inside. Dark walls painted grey with the coating color of sadness, lacking any energetic life. A dark shadow of hopelessness wrapped itself around him, a haunting reminder of the gloominess of prison life. This young man of eighteen years, with a slender body shape, was both fragile on the inside and outside, trapped in this environment of futility. It was as if he wanted to be heard, but there was no audience to listen to him. He was placed in captivity like an animal at the zoo, and he could not trust anyone. His lethargic movements showed a human being who had no desire to live. I could understand. A system of justice displaying no justice was a crime in itself. How could society allow young people to be treated in such an inhumane way? Who were the real criminals? Are their parents who abandoned them serving time for their crime of neglect? This young man received the punishment of prison, being the onlooker on his Graffiti-artist friends tagging trains, while his so-called friends fled the scene before they could be caught...

The police blamed him for all the damages. I became overwhelmed with anger at the thought of his unjust pain. I wanted to scream and shout at the world for this horror of life. Unfortunately, no sounds from within me could be heard. The tears from my eyes became the words of my anger and sadness toward this poor young prisoner. He leaned closer to me, as if he wanted to let me know that he felt my emotions of pain.

As I approached the young man who was sitting on a bench against the wall, his eyes met mine with a yearning for attention. All it took was the twinkle of his eyes, and I knew he understood the vulnerability of human life, the alienation of the human spirit, and the sensitive spirit of two lonely hearts who hear the beat of a different drummer. The beat of a confused, sensitive voice that is so alone in sadness, pain, terror, and solitary confinement.

As I moved closer to him, he started to turn away, as if he wanted to leave my world. But there was a hesitation in his movements. His lack of trust in a stranger was clear. I sensed a secret world of nightmares. I realized patience would be necessary in our relationship.

I glanced at my watch, realizing the minutes were passing too quickly. I realized an introduction was necessary. "I am your tutor," I said. I asked the student, "Do you find my presence uncomfortable?" There was no response except for the lowering of his head toward the table, as if a noose was leading his neck to a guillotine. I asked him, "Am I bothering you?"

The young prisoner slowly looked towards my face, directly into my eyes, and replied bitterly, "The world is bothering me. Society has condemned me to pay for a crime that I did not commit. Here I sit, my life withering away, as the sorcerer spreads his wings. The evil power that plots my destruction. Preying on human life. Committing more crimes on innocent victims. Dark clouds are weighing heavily over this earth. The storm of Death and Hatred is approaching. I am a victim of man's frustration. Self-destruction is my only salvation. My life is doomed..." He said this in a defeated way.

The sound of anger screaming from his voice, underscoring his words, shook my soul intensely. Something deep inside me felt his loneliness. He couldn't hide. The pain in his voice was calling out for help. I could hear him pleading for someone to listen to him, to help him find a better world, before it was too late.

I moved my hand slowly toward his face, noticing no movement in his eyes. Sullen, so forlorn. He was in a world galaxies away. Who would bring him so much pain? Why would anyone do this to such a beautiful human being?

As my eyes focused closely on his face, I could see the trembling of his skin scream out at me. It was as if the pain was trapped around his face. He was suffocating in it. Attempting to break down his formidable wall was frightening. The mortar had to be dramatically thick for these bricks to feel like masses of steel. The shattering pieces would leave their presence.

Did I have the right to walk through the corridor of his mind? To search the maze for the answers to my questions? Can he see me? Can he hear me? Can he feel my presence? Where were his thoughts traveling to? Are they floating or sinking? Will his unfathomable depth of soul dig a deeper valley? Will he lock the prison doors around himself, swallowing the key to his freedom?

Nervously, he looked up at me. He did not try to pull away. His eyes were a vision to behold. I saw a divine light burning, an artistic image embodied with soul. Never before had I seen such depth of character! He was yearning for something, searching for energy to allow his hidden domain to explode. I sensed that he wanted to share his world desperately with me. Unfortunately, his wall would not come tumbling down. In order to understand his world, I had to be patient.

He had been abandoned. He was vulnerable to the expectations of life. He wore the armor of defensiveness to protect himself from feeling any more pain from society. Yet I felt that he was divinely powerful enough to transcend my mind to a deeper level.

Part of his soul had been neglected. His suffering could no longer hide itself. I knew it was necessary for someone to take care of his soul. Allow him to believe in himself, to trust himself, to begin to find his true identity. To cleanse himself from the nightmares of his childhood. I wanted so dearly for him to dream of adulthood. I wanted him to trust me. I yearned for him to be my friend. I hesitated for a moment, and then asked him, "Are you angry with me?"

He looked at me hopelessly. "Anger comes second nature to me. It's been part of my personality for as long as I can remember. I'm not proud of it. It's as if the devil has planted his spell of wrath on me. Can you understand that?"

"Yes. Sometimes I feel this uncontrollable urge to lash out at people. I feel provoked. I don't know what overcomes me. I believe that if we are going to understand our relationship with the world, we must find some insight into this anger. There is a reason for a person's anger. Yes, it might be a very dark secret, but there is an answer to it. The most challenging part of my life has been to search the depths of my soul for those answers."

"I'm afraid to find the root of this evil," he said in a shy manner. "Scared of the nightmares that I will find."

"I was scared, too," I said. "Admitting your fears is the first step toward freedom. Please remember that. We are human beings with hearts full of emotions. Pain and difficulty can sometimes serve as a pathway to a new level of dealing with the obstacles of life."

"It's my dad," he said unexpectedly. "I hate him. I despise him for all the pain and suffering he has given me. He has embodied the devil.

Do you know how difficult it is to understand that my father is the enemy? He hates me as much as I hate him. I can't even stay in the same room with him without getting sick to my stomach. When I listen to him talk, laugh, cough, the sounds make me cringe in horror! I have nightmares of me trying to kill him. When I wake up, I feel saddened by the reality that he is not dead. Living my life with him has been pure hell. How could God allow this to happen? Has he no mercy on me?"

"Do you feel any love towards your dad?" I asked.

"Love, what is that word? That unimaginable feeling has never surrounded me or wrapped itself tightly around my being. Why would I love him? All he ever did was blame me for being alive, for being his son..."

"What do you mean, 'blame'?" I asked as his voice trailed off.

"If I was a minute late for school, spilled my milk, forgot to shut the door, he beat me. Beat my body, beat my mind, and beat my soul until there was no hope left. The candle of light stopped flickering. I wish I could still see the light of hope. There's no hope with my dad."

"But there is hope inside your soul. The most important person in your life should be you. When you don't believe in yourself, then you will be defeated. You must remember that no one can take away your freedom of trust in yourself. No one can strip you of your inner self. Not even your dad. It's too bad that your father can't support you."

"How can my father support me when he can't even support himself? He's an alcoholic. He would always come home drunk, ready to attack one of us. He would scare me by the irritable and angry mood he was displaying. One wrong move, and I was doomed—"

"Doomed?"

"Doomed to darkness. A world full of nightmares. My nights were always sleepless. I can remember the same nightmares over and over again."

"Can you share them with me?" I asked.

"I have this reoccurring one about an art project that I did at school. The painting is torn into pieces and set on fire by someone from the Ku Klux Klan. Then all the papers are scattered everywhere. I am desperately trying to catch all the pieces. Trying to hold onto them. Wanting to put the pieces back together, as in a puzzle. When I suddenly wake up, I'm shaking, shivering, totally lost in despair. Confused... frustrated... helpless..."

"Your dreams or nightmares show the depth of your soul. You are feeling scattered, not focused. You want to move forward with your life, but the anger towards your dad and society scatters your mind into confusion. You want your creative spirit to unfold itself, to be the focus of your life, but someone or something is holding you back—possibly your father's approval, or maybe even society's. Was there a situation in your life where your artwork as an artist was not approved of?"

There was silence for some time. I could almost hear the pain surrounding him. Minutes seemed to pass into hours. I wanted to reach out and touch his hands. Reach out to his painful world. He was galaxies away. His eyes were suffering. His thoughts and passions were struggling to be heard. He was suppressing a desire in his heart. This unexpressed passion demanded some kind of release or expression before it exploded into destruction.

I finally broke the silence. "If we don't explore the soul's power, we become its victim. We suffer instead of evolve. If we hold these thoughts and passions of ours inwardly, then they will stir up problems within us, creating unsettling thoughts that can turn into an illness. Thus, we become disconnected from life."

Suddenly, the words poured out of his mouth as a waterfall from above. His visual presence looked like a bird that had just flown out of his cage. "When I was fourteen years old, my English teacher encouraged me to enter a writing contest. I was hesitant at first, but with her insistence, I decided to. I was elated when the school notified me that I had won. With my uncontrollable excitement, I ran home to share the good news with my dad. He grabbed the paper from me, harshly looking at it with eyes filled with disgust. I could see the verdict of his judgment. He tore the paper in miniscule pieces and yelled that I was late from school. He told me to clean up the mess of papers. I saw the words of my work fly around the room, trying to find a place of solace. Instead, they landed firmly on the ground; it was as if my body had been gunned down with the blood splattering everywhere. My lifeline of wisdom was abandoned, just as he abandoned me. I HATE HIM!"

I could see the tears of sadness and pain. But I could also see hope. If he had an image of himself as an artist, maybe he could forget his inferior feelings and concentrate on his creative spirit. Suddenly, I saw a beam of sunshine within this young man. A light of hope; a candle of light.

All I could say was, "I'm sorry. I'm sorry that your father does not understand you. I hope, in time, you will see that I do understand."

His eyes showed a glimmer of hope.

the woods

Magical things happen in the presence of nature. Henry David Thoreau felt the importance of solitude through his encounter with Walden Pond. He believed that the materials of life become so self-absorbing that we forget about a higher presence. His soul became rejuvenated by the surroundings of "free" air. He was able to find peace of mind that no one could take away from him. The woods brought him a new level of consciousness.

I thought to myself, was it possible to create a situation at the prison where my student and I could receive an intimate contact with nature that would allow us to create new energy in our souls? If we could bond to this unpredictable beauty of nature, the presence of soul would blossom. There were many places to walk—to smell the air, see the colors of the rainbows and the trees and flowers—that would nurture our souls.

Once we could walk along the mysteries of the unknown world, our creative nature would permeate through our souls. Deep in thought, our souls would stir, bringing along a beginning of new hope, a light of sunshine. Breathing this new air would be exhilarating. A new existence would bring freedom of choice and freedom of beliefs. The unimaginable world would become imaginable. Taking care of the soul is taking care of nature. Even the Roman poets respected the mysteries of the soul through nature. We must respect the poetics of our souls by holding hands with nature.

To understand and take care of our hearts, we must understand and take care of the sky and earth. Solitude of lightness and darkness can surround our inner world if we invite nature to our calling. These gifts of nature bring forth the depth of soul, the poetics of soul. The lure of clouds as they approach us will allow us to grow closer to ourselves. If we want intimacy in our lives, then we must obtain the presence of soul in our lives through nature.

If we try to live without the presence of nature, our individual world will rot. Our lost soul will overpower us, leaving us out of touch with the spirituality of life. The mysteries of ourselves will rot away. Unfortunately, our modern world has lost its connection to our inner world, resulting in a division between Life and Soul.

Nourishment for the soul grows from simple seeds that germinate and blossom into a beautiful existence. This can be found in the simplest of daily activities. We must encounter the lost appreciation for the poetics of ordinary life.

To be able to walk through the woods nourishes the soul. To be inspired by the tall trees lifts our spirit into a new level of consciousness. The mysteries of nature bring forth an unknown world full of unconscious elements, things we encounter every day but take for granted. The mysteries of the soul are deeply rooted with emotions. These plants should be cherished.

As I looked at the prison and the walls surrounding it, I saw an abundance of color. The sun allows the rainbow to show off its color, illuminating the building as a place of reflection. The hills surrounding the prison can deeply affect us. They can bring forth a deep, emotional focus to a person's life. Nature and prison can bond together as a new source of energy.

I asked the guard if it would be okay to work with my student on the grounds of the prison. He hesitated at first and then reluctantly agreed to a short amount of time. Time was on the guard's side but not my student's. Who is he to judge the amount of time two people need to grow together? Only nature's calling would beckon us to the realities of time.

I met Clint at the foot of the hill. I could sense a peaceful manner within him. When he saw me, he turned away and reached down for a piece of dirt, which lay comfortably in his hand. He said, "A piece of dirt should be hidden inside each of our souls. If we are going to understand ourselves, then we must understand the simplicity of this earth. We tend to take this earth for granted."

I agreed. "We are numb to this world. We have lost the connection of home and family. There is an emptiness in our society. When we see the homelessness of the streets, we are viewing the deeper homelessness of feelings in our hearts. We have depersonalized ourselves. We have created this homelessness from the roots of our soul. A lost soul. We are wandering around aimlessly with no focus or direction. We are abusing ourselves by neglecting our inner feelings, the truth of our souls. If we wander back in time to the Greek mythologists, we would learn how to think more deeply and create more imaginatively. The Greek poets shared with the world a story so deep that these feelings could be shared with the world today. During this enlightened period, the mysteries of soul brought forth an imagination of poets that has formed the foundation of our lives, stimulating our deepest roots."

He looked at me, pondering. "Imagination is very difficult to express in a world full of anger, violence, and structure. The walls of society have suffocated the free spirit of the Greek philosophers."

I said, "The walls within yourself have suppressed your true desires. I can tell that these yearnings have been stifled for a long time. The truth of your being has been masked. This alienated society has supported this. You must not succumb to this devastating power or oppressive force. You must begin to see the poetics of everyday life. If you enter into the world of taking care of your soul, the distinction between lightness and darkness will blend together. The candle of light will enlighten your soul."

Suddenly, the sunshine became so powerful. Clint's eyes began to shine so brightly. It was as if a whole new world had arisen for both of us. A world full of hope, creativity, and wealth of energy.

"How does one begin to see the poetics of life?" he asked.

"By beginning to believe in yourself. To see the beauty within your soul. To search within the deepest valleys of your soul for the creative nature. This power of soul stems from an unknown source. It is secretive, if you allow it to be. Soul's work can be magical. We must find the courage to explore this wonder. Can you hear the music of the wind in the trees? Listen. The crickets, the church bells, and the whistling of the wind are calling us to feel the freedom of our search. Nature beckons us to have compassion for that possession that is truly ours, our creative soul. Look at the prison building as full of strong imagery. Look at the architecture as the hands that built it and the minds that created it. Then we can apply our imagination to the simple possession of life. Thus, thinking more deeply of the poetics of life."

I pointed towards the pond and said, "Look at the pond over there."

He walked towards it and stood in front of the grassy edge. The pond of water was still. I asked, "Can you see your reflection in it?"

He was silent. His eyes displayed a deep pain.

"Please, look at yourself. Find yourself. Find the piece that is missing."

He looked at me, smiling, understanding for a moment. Suddenly, he startled me with a splash from a stone that he threw into the pond. He laughed. I laughed.

He asked me, "Is life that simple? Can I find peace of mind through my reflection in a pond?"

"The key is to take care and be attentive of your soul. Whatever we find in the environment can feed our soul. We must take the time to investigate it. Nature is always calling us. Simple acts allow us to be simple with ourselves. We must return to the lost appreciation of the poetics of ordinary life. If we think about our everyday existence as if everything we do has a shadow of imagination surrounding it, then life will be more precious as we spread this creativity around us. The depth, insight, and wisdom of Greek mythology will permeate us."

He said, "How can anyone tell me how to live my life? My life has no purpose. There is nothing for me to look forward to. Every time I start to feel good about myself, society and my family drag me down into the depths of devastation. Why should I search for my poetics of soul when, sooner or later, someone will take them away, eventually taking my soul away?"

I said, "No one will ever take your soul away. That is yours. Trust can allow you to believe in yourself. Allow your soul to hear its voice. The voice will become so loud and clear. Allow yourself to be heard. When there is room to hear your voice, your soul becomes more spacious. Traveling with your creative nature will transform your mind to a level closer to the stars. You will clearly see a cosmic vision. Solitude will bring forth this transformation. The enchanting lure of creativeness will inspire you to be who you truly are and want to be. Be patient. There can be melancholy with your search. Stretching your soul can be painful. It will be a struggle at times. Try not to avoid it. The pleasures and rewards are unimaginable. It will ignite your fantasies. Your emotions will be as high as the clouds. Respect this care of your soul, and your soul will care for you. As the river rises and rushes down the land, run with it, play with it. Your individuality will rise from the depths of your soul. Depression will allow its own insight. Moods belong with the planets. They are part of you." I sensed that Clint was absorbing my words by the intense look on his face.

I continued. "Retreat from this world. Find a place of solace. Begin the journey of self-enlightenment. Nourish your soul with your writings. Even five minutes a day can cleanse you in such a creative way. Reflect, talk, walk, share. Journaling, dream work, poetry, creative writing, and painting will allow you to explore images of your life. You need to visit these passions. As you look around, you will see that your surroundings have a halo of imagination surrounding them. Don't chase your soul away. Invite it to stay for a time, a peaceful time. Nourish it. The soul needs life, just as the body needs food. You must understand that the unconscious elements of your inner world enhance you."

I paused, then continued. "Shelter will suppress the poetics of your being. Predictability stifles the spontaneity of life. Walk courageously down the valley of existence. Find a way to challenge yourself instead of feeling safe, dry, and unaffected. Show your presence. Leave this fast-paced world. Take small steps into the timeless zone of eternity. See the beauty of the moment. Capture it as a thief captures his prized possession. Hold it. Savor it. It will never dry up. Stir the soul. Open yourself up to its wonders. Become passionate. The soul thrives on warmth. It is the essential energy of the soul. Become. Affect yourself."

"How can a simple person as me reach that level?" Clint asked earnestly. I continued. "Allow the sacred to be felt. As we see the variety of thoughts surface, our reflections will become deeper. Our art will flow profusely. Listen to the sounds around you. Sacred moments strengthen a poet's art. Free yourself of everyday, worldly concerns. Thus, your spirit will unfold. Muse, revere, wonder, and explore. As you write, you will see yourself moving into deeper thoughts. There is no end to meaning. Poetry will provide you with a panacea of vision, music, wisdom, insight, and depth."

He asked me, "Can you help me?"

"Finding a relationship with someone you can trust will help you. Trust will help you. I am your teacher. I can't tell you how to live your life. I can give you the tools to begin your own journey of soul. Remember that you must feel the soul reentering your life."

His eyes touched my soul with penetrating warmth. I found comfort. I had never experienced this feeling before. A craving for something. Something was missing inside me. A lost piece of my puzzle, the mystery of my life. I became uncomfortable.

I thought it would be a good idea if we changed our surroundings on the prison grounds. We hiked down to a thick, wooded area full of dead branches. He acted so respectfully around me. I had never met such a genuine person. He showed me a concern that warmed my soul. As I passed the branches, he assertively pushed them aside. I sensed he was a caring, tender young man who was concerned with how other people felt. He seemed concerned about my welfare. As we approached the sitting area of the log, I became overwhelmed with solace. It was as if someone took the stagnant air out of me, rejuvenating me with fresh air. I became vulnerable to everything around me; I wanted to stay there forever. His presence was so comforting to me. A spiritual friendship was beginning. From Clint's facial expression, I saw he shared those same feelings.

Days passed. Weeks passed.

The woods of Fullersburg were full of past and present. Every way you turned, there were leaves of every color. As we took our walks, I felt reawakened. I yearned for our times together. The student energized my soul. I felt hopeful for a more fulfilling life.

Unfortunately, the other prisoners could not appreciate the beauty of this world of hope that I had encountered.

The prison was built in the early 1900s. The community was not happy with this citadel. Conservatism prevailed in this surrounding.

Criminals did not belong in this town. As time went by, the prison became its own entity. Only the victims and loved ones of the prisoners could understand the meaning of prison life. Guilty or not guilty, these poor souls lived and died there, forgotten moments after their departure. No one would allow me to ever forget. Clint's sensitivity to life made all the prison walls collapse into pieces of a rainbow.

Our times together became the hope in both of our lives. The surroundings of the woods encompassed us into a safe world of comfort. I wasn't sure why the candle of light continued to burn, though I realized in time that the light would never lose its flicker. I could only feel the need to continue to inspire him to find some balance in his life. If there was an opportunity to nurture his artistic talents, I wanted to support this. My lessons encouraged Clint to write and draw about his feelings. Feelings were too difficult for him to express verbally. Painfully, tragically so. His sensitive approach to life was softening to my touch. I could feel his pain. I could feel his words trying desperately to speak. His pain did not allow this. He is a beautiful young man who has so much to offer this world. If only his family could have realized this.

The hands of time were in my possession. I sensed that he was a poet by his creative way of thinking. I reached out to touch his hand. He grabbed mine firmly. There were no words, only the poetry of feelings. A companionship between two spiritual people. I hoped he would share his poetry with me.

"Share some of your writings with me," I said.

"I've never read any poetry to anyone before. I'm a little nervous. My dad would always interrupt me. Whenever I felt that it was important to communicate with him, he would start yelling for no reason. I was his scapegoat. After many years of insults and humiliating remarks, I decided it was easier to keep peace. My mind became a haven for my poetry. The poetic thoughts became more prevalent as my father came around me. I never wrote down any of my words because I was afraid he would take away my sanity or freedom by physically abusing me. So I hid them tightly under lock and key inside my mind. Now the lock can be opened, for your spirit has calmed the fear inside me. You listen to every word that I speak. You allow me to feel important. As we spend more time together, I feel that my nervousness will fade away. My words will flow inside you. You will soon understand. You will travel with me to a world full of tranquility. A retreat of solace. A mystical life that no one will take away from us. No one, not even my father."

After he read from his journal, the echoes of his voice surrounded my mind as peacefully as a symphony orchestra performing Mozart. The crescendo of sounds enlightened my soul beyond imagination. His poetic words led me on a journey to a magical retreat of solitary confinement, where no one could release me. The romanticism of his language wrapped itself around me as a lover's embrace. The deepness of his voice reached the dark depths inside me, searching for my passion, the passion of creative souls who yearn for inner communication.

"You have enlightened my inner world. Thank you for sharing a part of your soul."

abuse

During the fall, the vibrant colors from the trees permeated the prison walls, creating a rainbow of hope. As the leaves fell, our times together lasted longer and were more frequent. Our layering of emotional protection began to unfold itself.

Clint began to talk about his home life as a child, his father's excessive drinking, the physical abuse while his father was drinking, and the rivalry between parents due to the effects of alcoholism.

As we walked around the grounds, viewing the beautiful fall colors, he asked, "Why does a bottle of alcohol have so much influence on a person's life? Why is my father so powerless over a drink? Why would he rather socialize with his booze than spend an hour with his son? Why would he hit me for no reason?" As he asked me these questions, I could see the abandonment of a lost child. A child who yearned for some attention from his father.

"Your father is an alcoholic who is powerless over alcohol. He has a disease that he has no control over. Every time he drinks, he will not be able to stop himself. I know this from going to AA meetings. My ex-husband is an alcoholic. An alcoholic has two choices: stop drinking and get support or continue to drink and lose many loved ones, including losing himself. That's why I am no longer married. My ex-husband continues to drink. I used to think I was crazy. He wanted me to think that I was to blame for all his irresponsibility. I finally realized that he was the one who was crazy. Unfortunately, the progression of alcoholism becomes haunting—loss of family, finances, and health. A funeral in the waiting."

His eyes would not look at me. He understood. Minutes seemed to turn into hours before Clint began to speak. Then his eyes searched the comfort of mine. "I hate my dad for what he has done to me. The hurt of abandonment is so painful that it keeps me up at night." Suddenly, he transformed himself into a victim of uncontrollable anger, an anger that could suffocate both of us. I didn't recognize this person. Pain surrounded us. I felt the wall between us rebuilding itself. I sensed his loneliness and isolation from society. "Why should I trust anyone?" he asked. "All trust ever gave me was more abuse. Who really cares about me? My father certainly does not. All he cares about is his bottle of booze. Then there is my mother. All she cares about is keeping him away from the bottle."

I could see how the abuse from alcoholism was so devastating to this young, creative boy. This act of victimization was damaging to his human spirit. There is no such thing as a willing victim. He is a child who deserved the love and protection of his father. His father can be seen as an individual who destroyed the innocence, trust, sensitivity, kindness, and humanness in another human being. This is called neglect of a child. This young soul had been denied an environment to express his love.

"You have had your trust so severely shattered. Your feelings are a source of great confusion. You are afraid to own them. You are afraid of another rejection. You are sick of all these violations, denials, and betrayals. A crime of violence has been committed against you, who is an innocent victim. Your father has violated trust, power, and protection."

Clint whispered, "I feel so lonely." He paused like the silence of the water at bay. I reached out to clasp his hand to break the silence. He continued. "I am always running from people. It's so difficult for me to communicate. My emotions feel frozen. I can't connect with people. All I feel is anger, hurt, pain, and isolation."

"I know this is difficult, but you must be able to find a safe, non-judgmental environment where you are free to express your thoughts, feelings, and reactions of your life."

"Where do I begin? It is so difficult and painful to explain the depth of fear and pain I constantly carry with me. It's all-encompassing in my life. It haunts my soul."

"It takes time. Time is your friend. To accept this fear and pain is a very important step in this process of recovery. It won't go away. Understanding it and finding ways to ease it will allow you to find happiness in your life. Your father's alcoholism will always be his disease. Until he gets help for himself, there is nothing you can do to change him. But you can change yourself. You don't have to feel crazy anymore. You can find safety in this world. You can find that feeling of belonging with others. You can find people to trust who won't lie to you. You can begin to love yourself. Love, protection, and nurturing can be found if you are willing to reach out for them. What has been lost can be found. First, you must know what you are looking for."

"I am looking for a safe place to feel good about myself. I want to like myself. I want to love myself. I want someone to love me. Love me for myself."

"Let's start now. I'll help you rebuild that hope. I'll show you the avenues you need to take in order to find the comfort, protection, and love that you deserve. Trust me."

His eyes looked so deeply into mine that I could feel a sensation of trust from him. The candle was flickering. There was hope. He was starting to believe in himself.

manic depressive

The leaves were almost gone from the trees. Soon, the cold dim winter would be upon us, bringing forth temperamental moods. Time was moving too quickly. I could sense that our times together would diminish, just as the leaves of the trees.

We became inseparable. Our minds, that is. We both understood the pain and abandonment of alcoholism. Sharing our loss of belonging brought us closer together, until a new dimension of Clint's life unfolded itself, an aspect of his personality that would add confusion to our relationship.

During our most recent visit, Clint's mood was depressed. Silence seemed like an eternity for me. His saddened look made me aware of his uncertainty. There seemed to be a power or spell controlling his mood. He was suffering. I saw a stranger who was unrecognizable. Darkness overpowered lightness. This outside force was at war with him.

I touched his face. He looked up at me as if he were in a trance. He asked, "Where do I take this pain of mine? I try to run away, but it stays at my side. Inside my soul, there are things that scream and shout. It's like a curse that haunts me. It holds me tightly, unwilling to let go."

I felt his nightmare.

"I was fourteen when I had my first attack," he said. "When the siege began, I lost my mind rapidly. My mind began racing in all directions. I was staying up all night. Partying with friends. I was a crazed animal. Nothing could stop me from living on high energy. I felt great. I could conquer the world, settle the challenges, and defeat the unconquerable. No compromises were necessary. Everyone and everything would compromise to me. Exhaustion was never reachable. The pace was exhilarating. Even my friends were amazed by the intensity of my behaviors.

"I could carry on endless conversations. My mind was my best friend. Who else could think as quickly as I could? I started to think something must be wrong, but I could not ask for help. Problems must be kept to myself. My dad would not understand. Even if I tried, he would not understand. He was consumed with his companion, alcohol. My feelings were so fast that I couldn't catch some of them. I tried following them. Many of them became lost in space.

"Euphoria overpowered me. I could do and be anything. It was a narcissistic feeling. I could capture a disillusioned audience. This overpowering presence brought out the bizarre. I became aimless. I did not need sleep. Sleep was the enemy.

"Then my mind had a hard time keeping up with itself. The circuits were crossing over each other. I tried to slow my mind down, but as hard as I tried, the circuits would not shut off. I became irritable and restless. I craved excitement. There was an urgency to my life. My mind became chaotic. My surroundings were an enigma. I became confused, disoriented, and scared. My mind became a battleground. I didn't recognize myself anymore. I looked in the mirror and saw this paranoid, violent monster. My thoughts raced through my mind so fast that I could not catch myself in the race. I wanted desperately to slow down. I begged for mercy. No one heard me. Only the voices of restlessness.

"People started having a difficult time keeping up with me. I undertook more projects than humanely possible. I couldn't concentrate in school. Sleep was dreadful. I felt as if there was a gun to my back that forced me to keep going. Life was impatient with me. I became impatient with life.

"Then the energy level became short-lived. I burned myself out. The bottom fell out of my life. Exhaustion overwhelmed me. Nothing of my life was clear. It was senseless. I would stare out the window, not knowing who I was or where I was going. I could not make sense out of anything. School was incomprehensible. The clarity of life was now a fog. A tortuous world surrounded me. My mind became the devil in disguise by mocking me, confusing me, depressing me. Life was no longer exhilarating. It was dreadful. I did not want to leave my room. I locked myself and my mind inside and threw away the key. No one could come into my life. All I could think of was death. I was going to die. Why should I live when life was so meaningless? Pulling myself out of bed was horrifying. If I decided to go anywhere, it was only because my friends and family forced me. Many times, my mom had to call the truant officer to get me to school. I used any excuse to get out of going. I hid myself under the covers. When they got me out of bed, I could hardly get my clothes on. I dreaded talking to anyone. I stayed by myself, alone in dread. The real world was no longer safe to me. My comfort zone was alone with thoughts of suicide. The thought of death was comforting.

"I sat at school, dead. My mind was mindless. The students started making fun of me. They didn't understand the pain, anger, disorientation of my soul. My only friend was my depressed and disillusioned mind. When I awoke, all I saw were nightmares of reality. I went to sleep to hide from them. There were more nightmares that haunted me in my sleep. I would only think of death as a solution. The comfort of death sounded soothing. To escape from the world was the only answer, so I could release these chains from my soul. All I could feel was total despair, hopelessness, and horrifying thoughts. I could no longer follow the path of my own thoughts.

"I thought I was crazy. My mind was burning itself out of existence. Useless. Insanity was surrounding me. Can you imagine not being able to enjoy life? Can you fathom not being able to think or talk normally? It grips you so badly. The night terrors. The day terrors. Maybe the only satisfaction is knowing what it feels like to be old, sick, and dying, where there is no hope, no laughter, and no pleasure. I was so frightened. I wanted to be myself again, hopefully soon. But I knew I wouldn't.

"Then my mood would change again. I would feel enthusiastic, working hard again. These exhilarating moods were very seductive. I enjoyed them. They filled my mind with an insurmountable amount of ideas. I felt as if I could do anything. They were intoxicating moods followed by depression. An unpredictable madness would take over."

I sensed this out-of-control feeling from Clint. His hands were sweating. "How long did this roller-coaster situation last?" I asked.

"Some weeks I would be impulsive, chaotic, energetic, and crazy. Other weeks I would be withdrawn, desperate, suicidal, doomed. Where was my reality? Whom could I trust? I could not trust myself. Only the devil could."

I asked, "Did you ever get help for your illness?"

"No. The only help I wanted was suicide. Where could I take this pain of mine? Every time I ran, it would be by my side."

"There is help for you. You have a mental illness that does not have to control you. You have manic depressive illness. It is believed to be a genetic disease. You are not crazy. What you have expressed to me is part of the illness. You are not alone with this disease."

Clint could not believe his ears. "Are you telling me the truth? Can I truly find peace in my life again? Maybe I am not crazy. Is there a chance for me to be happy again? I am beginning to feel my depressing thoughts leaving. You are providing me hope, the hand of trust. You are protecting me from the hurt and pain of my illness. You are bringing forth passion in my life."

I could see the sparkle of hope in his eyes. I put my arms around him and hugged him tightly. He held me tightly.

"I will be gone for a few days," I said. "I want you to write about your illness. It will help you. Would it be okay to contact one of the psychiatrists that I know in town?"

Clint did not know what to say. This would be hard for him since he did not trust anyone else. I could see the scared look upon his face. I realized that I would have to be patient. He grabbed his journal tightly and walked away without a backward glance.

hope

The colors of the leaves were fading. The leaves were almost gone. Our conversations became more enlightening and less darkening. His eyes showed the zeal as days went by. I knew that his sessions with the psychiatrist were helping, and I knew the medications were improving his mood swings.

As we spent more and more time together outside, our days became one with nature. When he looked at me, his eyes were filled with soul. I reached out for his hand. He held mine tightly. As he squeezed my hand tighter, I saw the innocent victim being lifted by his creative soul. Clint was trying desperately to hold on to the goodness of the earth. He looked into my eyes. He was at peace.

"Your inspiration for me to write and paint has been a Godsend. I realize this prison life is temporary. I will always live in a prison full of skeletons of the past and skeletons of the future unless, once and for all, I am released from this haunting nightmare. I am ready to leave and live a life of creativity. I have only a few weeks left here, and then my creative journey will begin in the outside world. You are a tender reminder of what hope is left for this world. A guardian angel of love for the forgotten. Keep spreading your wings so other people's nightmares can be turned into dreams, and the prisoners can find hope."

Tears began to wash the surface of my face. I could no longer hold on to the strength that I once had. The stream of tears continued. I was sobbing like a little child who had lost her mother; my happiness for him was uncontrollable. As I left that day, I found myself gazing at some of the few leaves left on the trees.

change of seasons

could not sleep that night. I decided to leave for work earlier than usual. The sounds of the leaves beneath my feet were a reminder of the ending of the season. I could not stop thinking about the special spiritual relationship that Clint and I shared. I was filled with elation for Clint and his new life.

Life is a reminder of how short our precious times can be. Take the moment in hand and hold on to it tightly, for tomorrow may be lost. I kneeled down on the ground to pick up one of the last fallen leaves. I held it tightly.

the candle of light

od grant me the serenity to accept the things I cannot change, courage to change the things I can, and the wisdom to know the difference...

As I finished lighting the menorah candles, I grasp the strength from this fire to understand the atrocities of these creative souls. Though the day is filled with darkened spirits, the light of the candles have illuminated shadows of warmth to my soul. The glow of the flames provides me hope for the other creative young souls of tomorrow. Why are innocent, creative young people abandoned by their families and mistreated by society? Has another Holocaust occurred within our society? These children are victims who were only searching for understanding, support, and love.

Clint was released earlier than scheduled from his prison stay. Fortunately, Clint was accepted to the junior college close to his home and is majoring in creative writing and art.

As for myself, I continue to tutor students, though my new journey includes taking classes to learn more about my inner yearnings. Presently, it is such a joy to be able to spend more time taking time for myself and searching the depths of my soul to find the answers. I must continually remind myself that I cannot neglect who I am and where I am going. I must continue to respond to what the soul presents to me, its fantasies and yearnings. If I don't, I will neglect myself.

I must allow the soul to follow its artistic pathway. Stifling this will perpetuate the unconscious world of ours. If there is no artfulness of life, then there is a weakening of soul. The avenue to transcend this mundane world is to practice a spirituality of soul, searching deep for the creativity within us all.

As I struggle every day for an enlightened moment, I will meditate and pray. I will find peace of spirit by examining myself for who I am, not who I wish to be. I hope this will bring forth an artful awareness of life.

I need to share with society that art is indispensable and can create a beautiful, serene world where talented souls can flourish. Our society lives in an empty environment due to the lack of an art identity. When creativity becomes a source of energy for our culture, the beauty of our souls intensifies. Our exploration of knowledge within ourselves will revitalize us.

We need to take time for creative thought. Our society lives too quickly. We must pause, search, explore the valleys and the peaks for endless possibilities to our lives. If we would take the time to reflect, our souls would be nourished with creativity. We need to take the time to know each other, spend time learning the creative aspects of our souls. We would feel more intimately connected if our lives would have a more enriching existence.

As we explore, our environment must include nature. Nature's touch will strip any façade away, leaving the depth of our souls. We must not be afraid. We must look forward to this new beginning, this magical richness.

It will be a challenge to search for our poetics of soul. It is necessary in order to feel the underlying forces of our being. It may not be easy to find these places and look them straight in the eye. Sometimes the most frightening work is the most rewarding. Peace can be found.

If we take time to write, paint, listen to music, and read, then we can transform our lives to a higher level. These gifts can be left for other generations to appreciate. As we create art, we are sharing with the world our deepest thoughts. These thoughts can be alive in the past, present, and future. There is no sense of time in the creative aspect of our soul. Peace is all we ask for. We can learn from the great poets, such as Keats. Our souls can continually evolve without the power of time. This gift of imagination can erase the mundane, rational, everyday existence. We can look into the eyes of others and see the passion that stirs beneath our exterior.

We must take care of our soul. Live deeply. Live passionately. Live creatively. Live imaginatively. Live with expression. Live with moods. Live with fantasy. Live with emotion. Respect our yearnings for exploration and not deplore them.

We need to understand who we are. We must become visible, not invisible. We need to love more of ourselves. We must accept imperfectness. Perfectionism is an illness. Searching for the unknown, questioning it and respecting it, will allow us to grow. We must accept our individuality and our unconscious behavior. Our fantasies should live.

If we can live from the heart of the soul, then our attachment to reality will become deeper. We will no longer feel confused or lost. We can begin to trust and believe in each other again. The pain of distrust will be forgotten. We must be faithful and truthful to ourselves. Look inside the crystals of life and gather the precious stones that we need to live a fulfilling life. We must appreciate this luster and brilliance of color as the clarity of our souls.

epilogue

eople who have bipolar disorder are among the most imaginative and gifted personalities that we as a society have.

Manic depressive illness appears to be the most genetic of the major psychiatric illnesses, and one most definitely linked to creativity. There has been extensive research showing a higher rate of mood disorders in artistic populations than from chance alone. A relationship does exist between depression, mania, and the artistic experience.

When there are periods of manic intensity interrupted at times by depression, a unique insight into the depth of human feeling is displayed. In these states, the mind grasps its hands in poetry, painting, and music.

During a manic state, symptoms of inflated self-esteem, overflowing energy, less need for sleep, and sharpened senses allow an unusual amount of creative thinking and increased productivity. Mania brings forth ideas and associations. It creates energies and enthusiasms.

Melancholy moves in a different direction—a slower pace of thoughts, viewing sadness and the pain of depression, gazing inwardly. This produces poetic, philosophical, and religious insight. A depressed state allows the artist to persist in his journey of creativity. The artist's pain becomes an integral part of his or her motivation to create. This cloud of depression adds insight into the artist's work. The world of pain and trouble allows the artist to feel and suffer. An emotional condition creates a passionate soul, brightening the genius of minds.

As we look backwards to the past and forward to the future, a lesson can be learned from famous musicians, artists, and writers who have dealt with or who are dealing with the challenges of bipolar illness. They have inspired our world with beauty and creativity beyond belief. The list of these wonderful people is extensive, so I am only listing my favorite artists: Irving Berlin, Edgar Allan Poe, Georgia O'Keeffe, Virginia Woolf, Jimi Hendrix, Patty Duke, Vincent Van Gogh, Ludwig Van Beethoven, and Peter Tchaikovsky.

Today's artists who are dealing with bipolar disorder must continue to find ways of structuring their chaotic emotions and thoughts; finding comfort in the arts will allow them solace. Wrapping themselves in their words, music, and thoughts will protect them. Most importantly, they must seek professional help when their pain and despair become their enemies. A soul mate of creativity and therapy will allow the candle to continue burning.

about the author

Roz Long has taught and counseled high school and college students with mental disabilities for over 25 years. She received her master's degree in special education at the University of Illinois Champaign-Urbana Karnes Fellowship Program. Roz studied under Dr. Sidney W. Bijou, who was the pioneer in behavioral and developmental psychology.

Her pursuit in helping others led to a master's degree in counselor education and a certificate in addiction counseling.

She has dedicated a major part of her career to the support and advancement of the arts and continues to partner with not-for-profit organizations. She is the founder of many arts festivals and indoor art venues, including an art center. She resides in Elmhurst, Illinois, with her husband and has two grown children.

www.ingramcontent.com/pod-product-compliance
Lightning Source LLC
Chambersburg PA
CBHW050339290526
45785CB00006B/2558